Excuses, Excuses, Excuses . . .

For Not Delivering

Excellent Customer Service—

And What Should Happen!

Darryl S. Doane and Rose D. Sloat

HRD Press

Published by:

HRD Press
22 Amherst Road
Amherst, MA 01002
1-800-822-2801 (U.S. and Canada)
413-253-3488
413-253-3490 (FAX)
www.hrdpress.com

Printed in Canada

ISBN 0-87425-614-3

Cover design by Eileen Klockars
Editorial services by Robie Grant
Production services by CompuDesign

Dedication

•

To Mr. Joe Breniser and Mr. W. Roderic Covey for their guidance, mentoring, shared wisdom, and most important, the friendship they have given to us over many years.

•

To all the customer service and sales representatives who represent the front lines of so many companies and deal directly with the customer every single day.

CONTENTS

Introduction

Excuses, Excuses, Excuses for Not Delivering Excellent Customer Service—And What Should Happen!

This book is about everyday excuses we hear for not giving excellent customer service and how to shoot those excuses down.

A few years ago we were doing a meeting for a group of approximately fifty individuals at a well-known hotel in Cleveland, Ohio. Our presentation was part of a weeklong workshop and our particular portion took place on the fourth day. Now, these individuals were real coffee drinkers, having gone through three large containers, and they were in need of more. As an employee of the hotel was passing down the hall, one of the participants sitting in the back of the room near the door noticed him and said, "Excuse me, could we please have some more coffee in here?" The hotel employee had the opportunity to respond by simply saying, "Yes, sir, I'll have that for you in just a moment." That would have satisfied the plea being made and allowed for life to move along pleasantly. However, what actually happened is that the hotel representative reacted by saying, "You know I have four other meetings going on, three of my co-workers have called off today, one of our coffee machines is malfunctioning, and I'm not having my best day." Now, since our group had just been in the process of settling back into our session from a break, we all observed this moment of intense focus on so many items by this hotel employee except the one that critically needed his attention—the customer! We did not care about the other meetings. We did not care about those who didn't show up for work today. We didn't care that a machine was not working properly. We wanted coffee! We wanted service! Your customers want service! Excuses are those obstacles we ourselves create for not doing or avoiding those things we have an inherent responsibility to provide the customer with—excellent professional service in a caring, friendly, and consistent manner.

Deliver Excellent Customer Service and Stop Giving Excuses, or Be Prepared to Self-Destruct!

This book is for any company, business, or organization that deals with customers and has a passionate desire to survive. We've all been customers ourselves, and we're tired—tired of inadequate service, a lack of concern, and a take-it-or-leave-it attitude. We're tired of being told everything under the sun except that which we long to hear, "How may I help you?" followed by the appropriate action. But the time has come. The line has been drawn, and those wishing to remain in business must listen to the cry from the individual who must be the central component of any successful business—the customer.

We have all heard excuses as customers ourselves, and we know how very frustrating these moments are. We all want excellent service; and when we do not receive it, we will take our business elsewhere.

This book's primary purpose is to explain how to do away with all the excuses for not delivering the service we crave and what should happen to stop the excuses from ever happening in the first place.

> "Tell me what you can do for me, not what you can't do —and then do it!"
> *The Customer*

There Should Be No Excuses for Not Delivering Excellent Customer Service

Excuses do not mean that business comes to a grinding halt and that individuals are incapable of taking care of the customer's needs. How ridiculous! But excuses get in the way of creating and maintaining good customer relations—the kind of customer relations that bring cutomers back again and again.

So we offer here the excuses we all have heard far too often, and much more importantly, what to do about them. Here also are new excuses being used as a result of our participation in the information revolution and all the new technologies and changes supporting it. Putting these excuses to rest once and for all is our primary objective, because there should be no excuse for not delivering excellent service. So here they are in all their glory, hopefully for their final appearance, never to be heard again, replaced by excellent service, service, service.

EXCUSE 1—MY COMPUTER IS DOWN.

What should have happened: Let me take down all the pertinent information so that I may begin to process your order. May I please take your name and phone number? I will go check the stock, get the information for you, and call you back shortly. (Make certain that you do.)

Insights: When the technology fails, does that automatically mean that you are doomed to failure also, or can you creatively and professionally rise to the occasion while still maintaining your focus on the customer and delivering the service she expects? No matter how much technology you are surrounded with, you are a people-dealing-with-people business.

EXCUSE 2—THE VENDOR MADE A MISTAKE.

What should have happened: I'm going to call the vendor right now and check on this matter. I'll call you right back with a status report.

Insights: Tell the customer what you can do for him, not what you can't do. Being a professional means knowing when to take responsibility for the customer's concerns and stop "passing the buck."

"The buck stops here."
Harry S Truman

THERE SHOULD BE NO EXCUSES FOR NOT DELIVERING EXCELLENT CUSTOMER SERVICE.

EXCUSE 3—IT'S NOT MY CUSTOMER.

What should have happened: How may I help you?

Insights: We are all in the customer service business no matter what our official title within our organization. If the customer is not the central focus of each associate within your company, be prepared for a catastrophe because you're on a collision course with a very uncertain future.

EXCUSE 4—WE'RE SHORT-HANDED.

What should have happened: May I please put you on hold for a moment? *Or*, May I take your name and number and I'll call you back? *Or*, May I help you?

Insights: Don't let the customer know what chaos (organized or otherwise) there may be behind the scenes. Professionalism, professionalism, professionalism is the key. The customer's perception of reality is the reality you

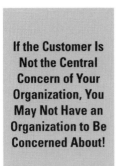

If the Customer Is Not the Central Concern of Your Organization, You May Not Have an Organization to Be Concerned About!

must focus upon. This perception of your business will be the deciding factor as to his continued use of your service or taking his business elsewhere. Give customers choices whenever possible. This allows them to feel that they have some control over the situation and they will tend to be more cooperative as a result.

IF THE CUSTOMER IS NOT THE CENTRAL CONCERN OF YOUR ORGANIZATION, YOU MAY NOT HAVE AN ORGANIZATION TO BE CONCERNED ABOUT.

EXCUSE 5—HE'S OUT TODAY.

What should have happened: He is unavailable; however, may I please help you?

Insights: Always offer your service to the customer. Let him/her make the choice to proceed or wait until the individual he/she originally spoke with is available. It is your responsibility to constantly educate the customer to the quality of the service you have to offer. Don't put off your excellent service, flaunt it!

Practice the Golden Rule

We're not talking about the one that says, "He who has the gold makes the rules." What we are referring to, of course, is "Do unto others as you would have them do unto you." And when dealing with customers, you need to go beyond the golden rule—"Do unto our customers as they would like to have done unto them."

We were speaking to a group of customer sales and service representatives and discussing with them moments when they themselves were customers and were treated the way they hoped they would be treated. When asked to share one word or a brief phrase that reflected those feelings, various responses such as pleased, happy, desire to return, satisfied, and so forth were given, but the one word that really shook us was *surprised*. How sad it is that good, quality customer service is at times so rare that when we experience it, we are surprised! We need to have our customers surprised every time they do business with us at the high quality of service they receive time and time again **with no excuses**.

EXCUSE 6—THAT PERSON IS ON VACATION.

What should have happened: He is unavailable. However, may I please help you?

Insights: May I help you? These are words you will hear again and again from us. We cannot emphasize enough the importance of giving yourself permission to take responsibility for the customer's problem, concern, or need. Don't let that opportunity slip away and lose that customer to never-never land. Seize the moment, and respond professionally.

EXCUSE 7—SHE'S IN A MEETING.

What should have happened: She's not available at the moment. May I take a message? *Or,* May I please help you?

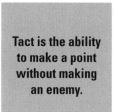

Tact is the ability to make a point without making an enemy.

Insights: Here we go again! Always offer your service to

---

the customer. Tactfully and diplomatically allow him to make the choice to proceed or wait until the individual he originally spoke with is available. It is your responsibility to constantly educate the customer to the quality of the service you have to offer.

EXCUSE 8—THE MANUFACTURER DID NOT RETURN MY CALL.

What should have happened: Sir, I've called the manufacturer with no response at this point in time. Please allow me to take responsibility for this situation. I'll continue to call the manufacturer until I do get the response we need, and I will keep you updated on my progress. Does that meet with your approval?

Insights: Don't play the victim. Take responsibility for the situation. When you anticipate the customer's concern, check with the manufacturer again and again until you do get the response you need for your customer. Even if you should still end up with a negative or even no response from the manufacturer, take it upon yourself to call the customer and give him a status report and tell him what additional actions you will be taking. Be prepared with alternative actions to resolve the customer's situation should the third party not come through. Remember that your goal is to fulfill your customer's needs! Don't build a bad image in the customer's mind of your suppliers; he is part of your service team.

EXCUSE 9—WE DON'T HAVE IT IN INVENTORY.

What should have happened: Let me check on that for you, and I'll get right back to you. *Or,* Would you care to hold? *Or,* May I get your name and number (if you haven't already identified the customer, company, address, phone number, and any other pertinent information) and call you back with that information?

Insights: If it is a service that you say you provide, you need to provide it. Here is where your team can play a critical role. "I" may not have the answer to this situation, but "we" have the answer. Tap the knowledge and resources of all the members of your team to resolve this situation.

EXCUSE 10—THAT'S NOT MY ACCOUNT.

What should have happened: May I have your purchase order number? I see that _____ was working on that for you. May I put you on hold for just a moment and transfer you to _____?

Insights: Should that individual not be available to assist the customer, be certain to offer your service to the customer. Let him make the choice to proceed or wait until the individual he originally spoke with is available. Take responsibility for the customer's needs. Also, be aware when you place a customer on hold for another employee to be certain that the customer does, in fact, make contact with that person. When you are the "first responder," you are responsible for that customer until he is in the care of another. Many customers are lost as a result of not following through to ensure they are being serviced. When you send a customer away, he will go away literally if he is not success-fully directed to the individual or solution he is seeking.

EXCUSE 11—I DON'T HAVE THE ABILITY.

What should have happened: Let me get that answer for you. May I put you on hold for a moment, or would you prefer that I call you right back?

Insights: This is another opportunity to tap the collective resources of your team. You may not have the ability, product knowledge, particular skill, etc., to assist the customer in that area but collectively the solution is there. Knowledge is something that is meant to be shared!

EXCUSE 12—I FORGOT TO CALL YOU BACK.

What should have happened: I'm returning your call. Thank you for calling earlier. How may I help you? *Or*, Here is the information you requested.

Insights: Take proper notes and messages with complete information and read them. Don't attempt to leave everything to memory. There is just too much informa-

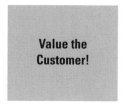

Value the Customer!

tion out there and accurate note taking is critical to be certain no details are overlooked.

EXCUSE 13—I HAVEN'T HAD TIME TO GET TO IT YET.

What should have happened: Yes, I'm calling to give you a status report on your particular request. Your order is very important to us and you should receive your items on _____.

Insights: If you don't have time for your customer, what are you doing as a customer service representative? It is an inherent responsibility to make time to focus on the customer. Make certain that you always do what you said you were going to do, and do it fast! Having an incredibly fast response time to your customer's requests is one of those items which will keep your customer coming back.

VALUE
THE CUSTOMER!

EXCUSE 14—I HAVEN'T LISTENED TO MY VOICE MAIL YET.

What should have happened: Yes, I'm calling to let you know that your order is ready, and thank you so much for calling and leaving your order on my voice mail.

Insights: The intention of voice mail is to enhance the communication process, not detract from it. If you have the privilege of using voice mail, please check it on a regular basis and respond to all your calls. It is not meant to be a screening device when it comes to customers. You should not pick and choose which individuals you will or will not do business with. They all deserve your most professional care. In many organizations voice mail is the main complaint for both internal and external customers when it comes to improper telephone techniques.

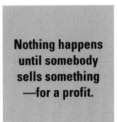

Nothing happens until somebody sells something —for a profit.

EXCUSE 15—MY VOICE MAIL IS FULL.

What should have happened: Thank you for calling earlier. I reviewed your message, and I've got some information to share with you.

Or, Please go ahead and leave your message, and I will get back to you shortly.

Insights: Be consistent in checking your voice mail and getting back to your customers. By regularly checking and responding to your voice mail you should have sufficient space available for customers to leave their messages.

EXCUSE 16—I'VE BEEN HANDLING SOMEONE ELSE'S PROBLEM.

What should have happened: You certainly called the right place. What may I help you with?

Insights: When you are focusing on a customer, give her your complete attention. Don't discuss other customers or their concerns. Your customer wants and expects your full attention and service. Treat every customer as if she is your only customer. Think what would happen if everyone in your organization on any given business day said, "Oh, it's only one customer, let her go." What a disaster that would be, with your company losing a sizable portion of revenue and most likely a great deal of future business.

EXCUSE 17—I WAS TIED UP IN THE PLANT OR ON THE FLOOR.

What should have happened: Thank you for holding. How may I help you?

Insights: Don't ever be too busy to pay attention to a customer. If you can't deal with a particular customer, be certain that the individual who is speaking with that customer gives him a variety of choices, including offering her assistance.

EXCUSE 18—I DON'T KNOW HOW TO USE THE PRICING BOOK.

What should have happened: May I put you on hold for just a moment while I get some additional information?

Insights: Don't tell the customer what you can't do for her. Focus on what you can do, and keep moving in a positive direction. Also, find the time to familiarize yourself with all the tools of your trade. An old cliche says, "If the only tool you have is a hammer, you're

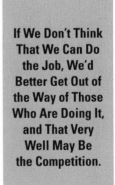

If We Don't Think That We Can Do the Job, We'd Better Get Out of the Way of Those Who Are Doing It, and That Very Well May Be the Competition.

going to treat everything as if it were a nail."
As old as it is and as often as you've heard
it, it's true! You should have as many tools in
your professional bag of skills as possible to
accomplish your primary goal of customer
satisfaction.

Check Out Your Work Environment

Everything counts! No matter how large or small the item is, if it assists you in getting the job done, it is important. Below is a list of items we have collected from numerous meetings with customer service representatives who were asked to identify the tools they need to have in their environment to be as effective and efficient as possible in dealing with their customers and assist in eliminating excuses.

Remember that these responses should only serve as a model for constructing your own list of essential tools which will impact your work environment in a productive manner.

- Computer
- Paper clips
- Phone/Headset
- Humor in the workplace
- Calculator
- Catalogs/resource books
- Fax machine
- List of phone numbers/internal extensions/phone books
- Listening skills

- Paper/notebook/forms
- Good technical knowledge
- Pen/pencil with eraser/highlighter
- Chair/desk
- Stapler
- Schedules
- Business cards
- Clean, efficient work area
- Waste basket
- Calendar
- Tissues
- Copier
- White out
- Post-it notes
- Good lighting/temperature
- Clock
- Great attitude

- **A Customer**

EXCUSE 19—THE PRICING BOOKS ARE NOT UP TO DATE.

What should have happened: May I put you on hold or call you right back while I check on some information regarding your order?

Insights: This is a perfect example of not having the correct tools in your work environment to promptly service the customer. It will take more time this way, but at least you are now concentrating on getting what the customer wants and not on an excuse.

EXCUSE 20—I DON'T HAVE A BACK-UP SYSTEM.

What should have happened: May I put you on hold while I check on some information regarding your order or call you right back? *Or, you may say,* I can personally take care of that for you right now.

Insights: You must realize that you are the back-up system. If anything stops, malfunctions, goes on the blink, gets disconnected, unplugged, zapped, or anything else happens, you must keep right on moving along delivering your excellent customer service.

EXCUSE 21—THE DELIVERY DID NOT COME IN.

What should have happened: I'm calling to let you know that we have checked the tracking on your order and it is _____ (or you can expect it at _____).

Insights: Take responsibility to show concern before the customer calls to check. You need to be able to anticipate your customer's concerns and needs. Remember, in the customer service business your business is fulfilling needs and becoming a solutions provider for those customers.

EXCUSE 22—I DIDN'T TAKE THAT ORDER.

What should have happened: May I please have your purchase order number so that I can access your order and assist you?

Insights: Excellent customer service is everyone's job. Assist the customer by taking responsibility for his concern. Be a Master at what you do!

Be a Master at What You Do!

As a professional, don't ever give yourself permission to have an I-know everything-there-is-to-know-about-my-business-or-my-customers-and-there-is-nothing-else-left-for-me-to-learn attitude. That's a very dangerous position to put yourself in. A true master realizes he or she must always be on alert for changes, new ideas, new insights, new ways to provide excellent service for the customer. When we get too comfortable, we often become complacent, take things for granted, and our skills begin to deteriorate. In order to become a solutions provider for our customers and an indispensable part of their business, we must continually work at knowing them as well as or better than they know themselves. This will place us in a position to anticipate change and fulfill needs while avoiding excuses for not delivering excellent service. When you achieve that level, you have attained a customer-responsive relationship which with proper maintenance will endure for years. Work hard to keep your customers, and it will pay off.

EXCUSE 23—WE HAVE A NEW COMPUTER SYSTEM.

What should have happened: May I please take your order?

Insights: The customer really doesn't care that you have a new computer system or that you may have brought three new people on board or that you have a headache. What the customer wants is for you to concentrate on him, worry about his needs, focus on his problems, and offer solutions. The customer wants a MIRACLE!

> You are constantly educating the customer to the quality of the service you provide and constantly differentiating yourself from the pack (the competition).

M-I-R-A-C-L-E

M—Make

I—It

R—Really

A—A

C—Colossal

L—Learning

E—Experience

EXCUSE 24—OUR DELIVERY DRIVER IS OUT.

What should have happened: How soon do you need that item? What would be a good time to deliver it for you?

Insights: Don't create obstacles to delivering excellent customer service. Deal with the customer's problem and don't add to it—solve it!

EXCUSE 25—DON'T YOU KNOW WHAT YOU WANT?

What should have happened: May I ask you a few questions so that we can deliver the exact item you need for the best value?

Insights: Don't ever come across as condescending to the customer. That can be a very

A TRUE MASTER IS NEVER SATISFIED AND NEVER TOO COMFORTABLE.

costly error. Accept the challenge before you while remaining professional throughout. Explore the mind of the customer by creating a dialogue with her. Ask open-ended questions that cause the customer to think more about the situation. These questions usually begin with who, what, why, when, where, or how and probe the mind of your customer. This allows the customer to talk more so that you can listen more to truly understand what she needs and how to solve her problem.

EXCUSE 26—THE CUSTOMER ASKED FOR THE WRONG PERSON.

What should have happened: May I please have some further information so that I may direct your call to the proper individual?

Insights: You want to be certain that the customer is dealing with the individual who will best address his needs and solve his problem. Always remember that person may be you.

EXCUSE 27—I'M TOO BUSY

What should have happened: May I please take your order?

Insights: Focus on the customer and his needs at the immediate time and let him know you will follow through with his order. Do not give the impression you are too busy to fulfill his needs. Ask for assistance from co-workers if necessary to complete the order in a timely manner. You can never be too busy to service the customer.

Provide On-Time Service

EXCUSE 28—WE MISSED THE 5:00 CUTOFF.

What should have happened: Here are a few alternatives I'd like you to consider so we may take care of your needs.

Insights: Let the customer know with no uncertainty that you are going to responsibly take care of the situation and fulfill her needs. When you start off with a negative comment telling the customer what was missed or cannot happen, you are planting seeds of doubt. The customer needs to believe in you. When you communicate doubts in your own capabilities, how can you expect others to reflect confidence in you?

What should have happened: Thank you for calling. How may I help you?

Insights: The customer wants service no matter what day of the week it is or what day we feel like it is. You need to get into that professional mode each time.

PROVIDE ON-TIME SERVICE AND DO IT RESPONSIBLY, RESPONSIVELY, AND REPEATEDLY!

You Can't Put It Back!

Take a tube of toothpaste and try this little experiment. For each customer excuse you have given for not delivering excellent service squeeze out an amount of toothpaste equal to what you would use to brush your teeth. Ten excuses equals ten squeezes, fifteen equals fifteen squeezes, and so forth. After you have recalled those excuses and have squeezed out the appropriate amount of toothpaste, try the following: Put it back! That's right, push it in, squeeze it in, whatever you must do, put it back! It's not very easy is it? Most people give up after a short period of time, realizing they really can't put it back without resorting to extra-ordinary measures.

When you give excuses for your service, or rather, lack of it, just remember that the spoken word once spoken is very difficult to take back and repair. Just like that tube of toothpaste, it's never quite the same again. It can be a real challenge and often impossible to regain the

trust and confidence you have lost with a particular customer as a result of the excuses you
allowed to slip out.

Deliver the service you know that you would
desire if you were the customer. Deliver the
service you know you are capable of presenting
to your customer. Deliver excellent customer
service and build a customer-responsive relationship to keep the customer coming back time
and time again, knowing they will not be getting
excuses but what they want—**service!**

EXCUSE 30—I'M ALL BY MYSELF.

What should have happened: May I take down
the information, your name, and phone
number, and I will get back to you with con-
firmation of the order.

Insights: Be sure to ask what the urgency is
and get back to the customer as quickly as
possible. Always have a fast response to any
inquiries or orders so you don't lose the
customer. When you say, "I'm all by myself,"
you are giving the perception to the customer
of not being able to help him, and he will take
his business elsewhere.

EXCUSE 31—I'M HAVING A BLANK MOMENT.

What should have happened: This is _____. How may I help you this morning (afternoon)?

Insights: Having a blank moment gives a non-professional image. You sometimes have to shake off what is causing the blank moment and get back into the professional flow. Do this before you pick up the phone or begin to speak to the customer.

EXCUSE 32—WE DIDN'T USE THE RIGHT SHIPPING.

What should have happened: What is the required time of arrival for this product? How do you feel about using ground shipment or is air needed?

Insights: Get the facts upfront for the customer's situation. Is it a breakdown situation? Is cost a factor in shipping terms? By asking the proper questions at the beginning when the order is placed you will avoid problems later.

Exploring the Mind of Your Customer

It's very important to view the customer's per-spective. You can get the customer to talk more while you listen more by asking exploratory questions (also referred to as open-ended questions) which allow you to probe the mind of the customer. These are questions that usually begin with who, what, why, when, where, or how. They make the customer (and you) think more about the situation and respond with more than a yes or no answer. This allows you to gather the appropriate amount of information required to understand the customer's problem and to become a solutions provider for that customer. It's similar to having a 5000-piece puzzle with only fifteen of the actual pieces. You do not have a clear idea of what the real picture is or should be. When you ask a customer the appropriate exploratory questions you are adding more and more pieces of that puzzle until finally a clear picture forms and you know exactly what direction you need to go in.

EXCUSE 33—HE ALWAYS CALLS FOR PRICE ONLY.

What should have happened: We would be very pleased to assist you and have you consider purchasing from us. What may we do to fill your order?

Insights: A customer who repeatedly calls in for a price or quote only can present a unique challenge. This individual has not been buying from you, yet you have been investing time in researching his concerns. You may need to ask questions such as: "What might we do to serve as more than a supplier of quotes for you? We would welcome the opportunity to do business with you." It needs to be a win/win situation for both the customer and your company.

Profit Is Not a Dirty Word

How long would you be in business without making a profit? Your customer knows that you have to be profitable to survive. You want your customer to win, but you must win also. "Nothing happens until somebody sells something—for a profit!" This is no joke, and a win/lose situation can put your company right out of business. Delivering excellent service with no excuses promotes the win/win for success! That "can do" attitude also promotes profit because your customers will return to those who produce results.

EXCUSE 34—THAT LAST CUSTOMER WAS A BEAR.

What should have happened: How may I help you?

Insights: Every customer deserves to be treated with the same respect and given the

---

same courtesy you would like to receive yourself. You cannot control a customer's behavior, but you can control yours if you choose to do so. Even when you have just dealt with an irate or angry customer, you owe the next customer professional service and she is expecting just that. If you just dealt with a particularly trying customer, take a deep breath, a short break, discuss it with a supervisor, whatever you personally need to do, but don't answer that next call or deal with that next customer face to face if you're "out for bear." A "What do you want?" or similar response to a customer will just move you toward a losing outcome. Instead, give yourself permission to respond to the needs of the customer in a pleasant, professional manner.

EXCUSE 35—MY CHILD IS SICK TODAY, AND MY THOUGHTS WERE ELSEWHERE.

What should have happened: Good morning. This is _____. How may I help you?

Insights: All of us at times have things that happen that will take our thoughts elsewhere—family concerns, an ill loved one, etc. Unfortunately, these are a part of life we all must deal with. As a pro-fessional you have a responsibility and challenge

Do What You Say You Will Do!

which you have accepted with your job and each day when you commit to come in to work. That responsibility is to be in your pro-fessional mode, ready and prepared to service the customer each and every time. While at your job it is important to give full attention to why you are there.

EXCUSE 36—OUR PHONE SYSTEM WAS DOWN.

What should have happened: Our phone system was down temporarily (or, we lost our phone service for a time). How may I help you?

Insights: Now, this is one of the few excuses you might actually verbalize since this could be a reality totally out of your control. We recently heard about some individuals working on a race car in a garage who forgot to remove the gasoline from the tank prior to their work on the car. The result was an explosion which miraculously did not kill

DO WHAT YOU SAY YOU WILL DO!

anyone; however, the building next door had its phone lines fried, and you guessed it, it was a service-oriented business whose phone lines were critical to the business. When they were up and running four hours later, there were many customers confused, upset, and wondering what had been going on. An explanation was appropriate, and getting back to servicing the customer quickly was priority one.

EXCUSE 37—I DON'T FEEL WELL TODAY.

What should have happened: How may I help you today?

Insights: Even though you may not feel well, the customer doesn't need to know that. Be as professional as you can be, and focus on the customer and not on your own situation. If you truly cannot function in a professional capacity, you should not be at work in the first place. You, as a professional, are a builder of bridges between your company and your customer. When you deliver excuses, you become a destroyer of those bridges which are critical to the survival of your company.

EXCUSE 38—I DON'T LIKE WORKING WITH THIS PERSON.

What should have happened: Take a deep breath, think a positive thought before proceeding, and be as pleasant as you possibly can be so that a positive image comes across the phone to the customer.

Insights: Nonverbal body language is recognizable even on the telephone. Putting a smile on your face will be reflected in your voice. One of the nicest compliments ever received is when someone tells you what a nice smile you have when you answer the phone. As a professional, accept the challenge of not always dealing with the most comfortable situation. You don't have the luxury of only presenting excellent service to those whom you prefer to deal with. You must treat every customer with the same professional courtesy, respect, and service.

EXCUSE 39—THIS CUSTOMER IS SO PUSHY.

What should have happened: May I ask you a few questions so that I can be sure that you get exactly what you need?

Insights: This is where your professionalism is really put to the test. It is so tempting to push back and escalate the situation to where you are almost certain to end with a losing result for both the customer and your company. We can't control how others react, but we can control how we respond. As a professional, you care enough to adapt and adjust to each and every customer. When you accept the challenge to remain professional with a pushy customer and give them the service he is demanding, it should actually be a brief encounter. As soon as he is convinced that you are focusing on his needs and taking care of his concerns, you should experience a pleasant change in the customer's cooperation level.

EXCUSE 40—THE SALESPERSON DIDN'T GIVE ME THE CORRECT INFORMATION.

What should have happened: Please give me the details of what you need, and I will assist you.

Insights: Put your focus on the customer and personally take responsibility for the situation. Use open-ended questions to obtain the

---

correct information so that you can service the customer appropriately. You should contact the salesperson to let her know about what has taken place. This could prevent future mistakes and uncomfortable situations of this nature.

EXCUSE 41—MY SPOUSE AND I HAD A DISAGREEMENT LAST NIGHT.

What should have happened: Good morning (afternoon). This is _____ . How may I help you?

Insights: Don't bring personal problems into the workplace. Be professional and concentrate on the customer. No matter how difficult it might be, talking about personal matters is not appropriate when dealing with a customer. She is there for service. You have an inherent responsibility to put yourself into a professional mode every time you deal with a customer.

EXCUSE 42—I DIDN'T UNDERSTAND THE URGENCY.

What should have happened: Do you have a breakdown? How soon do you need the material? When would you like to have this arrive?

Insights: Using the proper questions when the customer calls in to place an order will help to eliminate confusion and will determine upfront the details of the situation and its urgency. It is very important to determine a customer's needs so that you may respond accordingly.

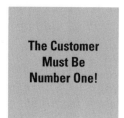

The Customer Must Be Number One!

EXCUSE 43—I HAVE A HEADACHE.

What should have happened: Mr./Mrs. _____, how may I help you today?

Insights: Don't answer the phone unless you are able to totally focus on the customer. Get permission to stay home if you are not feeling well. Coming to work when you are not able to deliver excellent customer service can be more costly to the company than an ill employee staying home.

THE CUSTOMER MUST BE NUMBER ONE!

EXCUSE 44—I HAVE TOO MANY PROJECTS GOING ON AT ONCE.

What should have happened: May I assist you by taking the information and checking inventory for you? I will call you back shortly with the answers you need.

Insights: Although you get very busy at times and may get overloaded, it is not necessary to let the customer know this. Look at being busy as a positive. If you didn't have customers,  you wouldn't be in business. The pace of business is not going to slow down and most likely will become even faster. A professional realizes this and invites it as a challenge to be met.

EXCUSE 45—WE HAVE A NEW PHONE SYSTEM.

What should have happened: What can I do for you today?

Insights: Know your system and how to use it. Take the necessary steps to get familiar with new technology as quickly as possible. Take notes, ask questions of your supervisor or whoever is responsible for teaching the skills of using the phone until you feel comfortable. If you do not know the system, you should not be on it until you do. Don't set yourself up for failure.

EXCUSE 46—MY OTHER CUSTOMER HAS A BREAKDOWN THAT I'M WORKING ON.

What should have happened: How may I help you? May I call you back with the information?

Insights: The customer doesn't have to know what you are working on. If you get to a point where time is a critical factor, ask someone else to help you by checking inventory for you and calling the customer back with the information. Always give the customer options and choices—never excuses.

EXCUSE 47—IT'S THE END OF THE MONTH.

What should have happened: Good morning. This is _____ . How may I be of assistance to you?

Insights: Wow, do we know what it is like at the end of the month. Sometimes you feel overwhelmed with reports and last-minute details that must be completed. Be a time manager and set priorities. Remember, priority one is your customer. There won't be any more reports to worry about or details to concern yourself with without that customer being attended to. We are talking survival here—your job, your fellow associates and their jobs, the very existence of your company! If you're not customer-centered and customer-focused, you won't have to worry about other items for very long. It will all be gone!

EXCUSE 48—I'M GOING ON VACATION TOMORROW.

What should have happened: Good afternoon. This is _____. What may I do for you today?

Insights: Whether your vacation is one day away or four months down the road your customer requires the same high quality service, and your vacation has nothing to do with that fact. It always seems like things build up just before a vacation is planned. Plan ahead and do a little each day to stay on top of the duties and projects of your job so that when the day before vacation arrives, you are

---

not jammed with last-minute details to handle. Take good notes and inform co-workers of orders, projects, etc., so they know their status. This will help to avoid delays with customers and also help to alleviate the work that may pile up before you get back to the office.

EXCUSE 49—IT'S LUNCH TIME.

What should have happened: This is _____. How may I help you?

Insights: If you are on a lunch break, do not answer the phone. Arrangements should be made in advance so that the phones are covered no matter what time of day it is or who is off doing lunch, or anything else for that matter. If you must answer the phone because of low staffing, do it professionally. The customer will get the feeling he is infringing on your time if you say it is your lunch time. You represent the company. Give a good impression and focus on your customer, not that sandwich.

MAKE THE CUSTOMER THE CENTER OF YOUR ORGANIZATION!

EXCUSE 50—I HAVE A LARGE ORDER TO PUT INTO THE COMPUTER.

What should have happened: Mr./Ms. _____, how nice to hear from you. How may I help you today?

Insights: It's great to have a large order! Time consuming? Yes, but look at it as a real asset. Learn the computer well so you can be quick at keying in the order. The customer you are currently talking to doesn't care

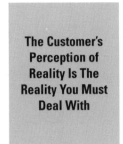

The Customer's Perception of Reality Is The Reality You Must Deal With

about your last order or how large it was. If you intend to do business with each customer, you had better give each of them the attention he or she demands and deserves from you at the appropriate time.

EXCUSE 51—HE'S AT A TRAINING CLASS TODAY.

What should have happened: _____ is learning how to service you even better today at a training session. How may I help you until he (she) returns?

THE CUSTOMER'S PERCEPTION OF REALITY IS THE REALITY YOU MUST DEAL WITH!

Insights: Training is a vital part of everyone's career. There never seems to be a perfect time for training to take place since it does mean taking individuals away from their posts. However, continuous improvement is an essential ingredient to survival. We never stop learning; we never stop growing and increasing our understanding of ourselves, our company, and our customers.

EXCUSE 52—THE SALESPERSON IS WITH ANOTHER CUSTOMER.

What should have happened: May I help you until _____ completes a transaction with a customer?

Insights: The customer knows he is not the only customer the salesperson works with. By offering to help him until the salesperson is available you will encourage the customer to consider working with other people within your organization.

EXCUSE 53—I DIDN'T GET THE MESSAGE.

What should have happened: I received your message, and your order is ready.

Insights: There simply should not be a message for a co-worker or fellow associate that is not delivered, received, read, or responded to. If you are the first responder, you have the responsibility to ensure that the message you take is delivered promptly to the proper individual.

EXCUSE 54—I HAVE BEEN OUT.

What should have happened: I received your message. How may I help you?

Insights: Don't focus on what you've been doing or where you have been. Instead, get right to focusing on the customer, her needs, her concerns. Customers appreciate a quick response time, so when you do return to your office or work location, check notes, voice mail, e-mail, all messages, and respond as quickly as you can. Should you be away for a few days or weeks, be certain to forward voice mail to another so that customers (internal and external) are not left in never-never land expecting a return to their message which is not coming.

Caring — Attitude

When it comes to delivering excellent customer service, there are a couple of critical items we would be remiss not to mention. They have to do with caring and attitude, that which differentiates the individual from the profession. It's the nurse at the hospital who takes an extra blanket to an elderly woman she observed was chilled and then raises her head to make her even more comfortable. It's the flight attendant asking if there is anything else he can do to make the trip more enjoyable. It's the customer service representative answering the phone with enthusiasm and an obvious desire to fulfill your need. It's the smile, greeting, tone of voice, proper use of humor in the work environment—it's bringing value-added and going beyond what is expected service.

When you call a company or go into a department store, bank, hardware store, you name it, you usually end up speaking with one individual. For all intents and purposes, as far as you are concerned, they represent everything that particular organization stands for. The perception you have of that person is the perception of service you will leave with.

Caring
+
a Positive Attitude
=
Excellent Customer Service
with No Excuses!

This is where each individual's personal commitment to excellence can make all the difference in the world. This is where each individual makes the decision about how much he or she will personally care about what he or she is doing and the person he or she is helping or if it is just a job and just another customer. This is where the attitude he or she owns, which permeates everything he or she does, will reflect a passion for excellent service and customer treatment which is vital to the very existence of the company. It all comes back to the individual and how responsible he or she has decided to be for his or her own actions. The team, the company, the organization doesn't control that. Each individual does. What's your personal choice?

Caring + a Positive Attitude = Excellent Customer Service with No Excuses!

It takes a fully functional independent "I" to be a member of a fully functional interdependent "we."

EXCUSE 55—MY BOSS IS NOT IN, AND I DON'T HAVE THE ANSWER.

What should have happened: May I take the information and get back to you with an answer?

Insights: The customer is interested in the bottom line. Do what it takes to get the correct and complete information to the customer in a timely manner. Never close the door to servicing a customer—you may never reopen it. Tell the customer what you can do and will do for him and then make certain that you follow through with those actions.

EXCUSE 56—THE SALES DEPARTMENT IS HAVING A MEETING.

What should have happened: May I assist you?

Insights: There are times when it is necessary to have group discussions or training or informative meetings. However, the customer is the one who pays your wages, so it necessary to give the service she needs and expects at the time she wants it. You can never afford to take your focus off the customer, even during training or a meeting to improve that very service. Years ago a young man was very excited about

You Must Have a Passion for Delivering Excellent Customer Service.

buying his first brand new car. Upon arriving at the selected dealership he was surprised to find that all the salespeople were nowhere to be found. A receptionist behind the main service counter informed him that, "Someone should be able to help you in about 45 minutes." The young man left, taking his business elsewhere. Meetings are important, but we can never take our focus off of that person who must be central to our organization —the customer.

EXCUSE 57—OH, I THOUGHT I WOULD HAVE REMEMBERED THAT!

What should have happened: May I please get that information from you one more time and verify the order?

Insights: Take notes! Repeat back the information for accuracy and completeness. Do not rely on memory for all the details. With all the everyday duties and business that take place, it is very difficult to remember all that the customer may say or all of the requirements of an order. When you do not remember what a customer has told you, you're spinning your wheels and wasting time by having to start from scratch again. When it gets done right the first time, it may take a little longer because of the attention you are paying to the customer, but the results are much more positive and actually save you time in the long run.

EXCUSE 58—OUR SHIPPING SCREWED IT UP.

What should have happened: May I check the status of that shipment and get back to you?

Insights: Don't place blame. Each person represents the company. The image you give is the image that customer sees of your company, not just you as an individual. Following through will catch many mistakes. Get in the habit of checking an order from the time it is taken to the time it is delivered. Take responsibility for the problem from the moment you begin to deal with the customer and focus on solutions, not who to blame for what has not happened. Accept the challenge and make it happen for that customer.

EXCUSE 59—IT'S NOT MY JOB.

What should have happened: This is _____. How may I help you?

Insights: Good customer service is everyone's responsibility in the office. How do you grow individually or as a company if you do not take responsibility? When an individual has an it's-not-my-job attitude, he or she is adding to the work, stress, anxiety, frustrations, and workload of everyone else. Besides, you never know when you may need that helping hand from a fellow employee. Eradicate the phrase "It's not my job," from your company's vocabulary.

EXCELLENT SERVICE EXCELLENT SERVICE EXCELLENT SERVICE

YOU MUST HAVE A PASSION FOR DELIVERING EXCELLENT CUSTOMER SERVICE.

EXCELLENT SERVICE EXCELLENT SERVICE EXCELLENT SERVICE

A Little Story

This is a story about four people named, respectively, **Everybody**, **Somebody**, **Anybody,** and **Nobody**. There was an important job to be done, and **Everybody** was sure that **Somebody** would do it. **Anybody** could have done it, but **Nobody** did. **Somebody** got angry about that, because it was **Everybody**'s job. **Everybody** thought **Anybody** could do it, but **Nobody** realized that **Everybody** wouldn't do it. It ended up that **Everybody** blamed **Somebody** when **Nobody** did what **Anybody** could have done.

— Anonymous

EXCUSE 60—HE'S AT LUNCH RIGHT NOW.

What should have happened: _____ is unavailable, but may I help you or may I take a message for _____?

Insights: The customer needs service and one individual's unavailability should not prevent that from taking place. Offer the customer choices and proceed based upon the customer's decision.

EXCUSE 61—THE DELIVERY SERVICE DIDN'T GET IT TO US YET.

What should have happened: I will check the delivery service and get a tracking number for you and call you right back.

Insights: When possible, stay on top of the status of the order and get to the customer before he has an opportunity to call you. Following up and monitoring the customer's order can prevent disagreements, mistakes, and irate customers.

EXCUSE 62—I DIDN'T TAKE THAT ORDER.

What should have happened: May I ask you some questions about your order so that I may assist you?

Insights: Gather the information and take responsibility for the order. Don't be unprofessional with your response by creating doubt in the mind of the customer as to how her order is being processed.

EXCUSE 63—IT ALWAYS TAKES THAT LONG.

What should have happened: Let me look into that for you and give you a status report as to exactly where your order is.

Insights: If it is taking too long to produce the service or item for your customer, it may be time to look at the process. Take action and let the customer know specifically what you will do for him and when you will do it.

EXCUSE 64—I'VE BEEN ON THE PHONE AND COULDN'T GET BACK TO YOU.

What should have happened: Here is the information you requested. *If responding to a message taken*, How may I help you?

Insights: Take a brief moment to call the customer in between other phone calls; and if necessary, leave a voice mail message to give the customer a status report so she knows you are working on her order. If you are responding to a message that was taken, be sure to get back to her as quickly as you can.

EXCUSE 65—I LOOKED AT IT, AND I DIDN'T THINK IT WAS RIGHT.

What should have happened: Let me verify your order with you for accuracy.

Insights: Get all the facts right the first time. Paraphrase and summarize your customer's comments and be sure you are both heading in the same direction. Have you left anything out? Practice active listening when your customer is talking.

Chances are if you don't know where you are going, you are probably going to end up someplace else, and don't be surprised when you get there!

EXCUSE 66—IT WASN'T MY PHONE, AND I DIDN'T KNOW HOW TO USE IT.

What should have happened: May I take a message?

Insights: If you don't know the system, just take a message; but be sure the call gets to the proper person, and follow through to be sure it is taken care of. By all means, learn the system! Get professional help when needed. The phone is the vital link to your customer, your business, and your profitability.

EXCUSE 67—ALL I DID WAS PUSH A BUTTON (THE PRICE WAS WRONG).

What should have happened: May I check that for you?

Insights: Look over your work for accuracy each time. This will prevent errors. Know your equipment, procedures, and system. Take the necessary training to become proficient. Pushing the wrong button could be very costly if the error is not caught. The great frontiersman, Davey Crockett, said, ". . . be always sure you're right, and then go ahead." These are still words that hold true when it comes to the way you treat your customers.

EXCUSE 68—I DIDN'T WAIT ON YOU.

What should have happened: How may I assist you?

Insights: You are waiting on that customer right now. Take responsibility for the opportunity presented to you and don't begin by closing the door to service. Open that door even wider and accept the challenge.

EXCUSE 69—THAT'S ANOTHER DEPARTMENT.

What should have happened: May I have your name and phone number and I will have that department call you, or would you like to be transferred?

Insights: It's a good idea to take the caller's name and phone number just in case the call would get disconnected. You will be able to pass the information on. Follow through to be sure the call is received by that department. Again, your involvement with the customer is essential to the successful completion of the transaction.

EXCUSE 70—I DON'T KNOW WHO TOOK YOUR CALL.

What should have happened: May I have your name? Your company is? Your order number is? Let me check that for you.

Insights: Don't lose a customer by not asking the proper questions. Identify who they are, what they ordered, and then follow through to find out the status of that order.

Do Whatever It Takes to Service the Customer!

DO WHATEVER IT TAKES TO SERVICE THE CUSTOMER!

EXCUSE 71—I PLAYED TENNIS THIS MORNING.

What should have happened: Good morning. This is _____. How may I help you?

Insights: The customer does not care if you are tired or what your outside involvements may be when he is requesting customer service. Put yourself in the customer's shoes before you give a nonprofessional response. No matter what games you play there are rules to be followed and the game of customer service is no exception. If you're not playing using the proper rules, you'll find yourself on the outside looking in. When you place yourself in the customer service arena, lead it with excellence, not excuses.

EXCUSE 72—I'VE BEEN OFF WORK SINCE WEDNESDAY, SO BEAR WITH ME.

What should have happened: Thank you for calling. How may I help you?

Insights: Take a few minutes at the beginning of the day to get back into the work mode and review what has happened since you were in the office. Your time off should not reflect time your customer must wait for responsive service.

EXCUSE 73—IT TAKES A WHILE TO GET BACK INTO THE WORK MODE.

What should have happened: Good morning Mr./Ms. _____. What may I do for you?

Insights: Give the customer your full attention. Focus on her needs and identify why she is calling. Get into the work mode prior to dealing with the customer, not during or after which may be too late.

EXCUSE 74—MY CO-WORKER WAS ON THE PHONE, AND I COULDN'T RECEIVE YOUR FAX.

What should have happened: Will you please send the fax over right now so that I can respond to your request immediately?

Insights: Using the same line for a fax, phone, or the internet can complicate matters. When possible, put each on a separate line. If this is not possible, be sure to give a time when you can receive the fax and be sure the line is open at that time.

EXCUSE 75—IT WASN'T ME. I DIDN'T TAKE THAT ORDER.

What should have happened: Please give me your purchase order or more information, and I'll take care of it.

Insights: Have a team attitude and a customer-responsive attitude. Cooperate with the customer and your co-workers by taking responsibility for the customer and fulfilling the need.

Take reponsibility for your customer, your own actions, and the consequences of those actions.

EXCUSE 76—THE VENDOR HASN'T GOTTEN BACK TO ME.

What should have happened: May I check with the vendor on the status of that shipment and get back to you?

Insights: Placing blame does not solve the problem. Get the information and find out the urgency and tell the customer you will get back with him as quickly as possible with a response to his question. Make sure the vendor knows the urgency when you place an order with her.

WHERE WOULD YOU BE WITHOUT YOUR CUSTOMERS?

EXCUSE 77—I'M ON BREAK.

What should have happened: How may I help you?

Insights: If you are on a break and there is adequate staff to answer phone calls, do not answer the phone. If you have no choice but to answer, then do it professionally without letting the customer know you are being interrupted. If you consider a customer request an interruption, you most likely will not have a business to have interrupted for very long.

EXCUSE 78—I'M SORRY, I'M WORKING ON A BREAKDOWN.

What should have happened: This is _____. How may I help you?

Insights: Get the information and ask the proper questions. Have a co-worker assist you if you cannot fulfill the request within a reasonable time. This is where the talents of the entire team need to be tapped. Don't ever close the door to business.

EXCUSE 79—I DIDN'T RECEIVE THAT MESSAGE.

What should have happened: May I ask you some questions? Could you please help me to understand the situation?

Insights: When there is no other choice but to start from scratch with a customer request, do so quickly and professionally. Try to determine where the glitch in service occurred. However, do that after you have serviced the customer. That glitch in service is not the customer's problem, it's yours.

EXCUSE 80—I DON'T KNOW HOW TO DO THAT.

What should have happened: Can you hold while I check on that for you?

Insights: Get help from a supervisor or associate so that you can give the customer excellent service. Perhaps "I" don't have the answer, but "we" have the answer. Don't overlook the resources available to you.

EXCUSE 81—I WAS BURIED AND JUST GOT TO YOUR MESSAGE.

What should have happened: How may I help you?

Insights: Buried or not, it is not professional to say this. Take a moment before answering the phone or dealing with a customer in person to clear your thoughts and then proceed with the service. You can never be too busy or too buried in other work to not pay attention to a customer.

EXCUSE 82—COME BACK LATER. I DON'T HAVE THE EXPERIENCE TO HELP YOU.

What should have happened: May I take the information and have someone call you? *Or,* Let me get _____ for you. He (she) is our expert in that area.

Insights: Always use your resources. If you have a co-worker who deals with the subject on a regular basis and has expertise in that area, ask him or her to help you or the customer in order to service the customer quickly and efficiently. Also, use this as a learning experience—keep notes on how the situation was handled so that if it comes up again you will be able to refer to them.

EXCUSE 83—I'M JUST HERE TO WATCH THE DESK.

What should have happened: How may I be of help to you?

Insights: Always be prepared. Take the opportunity to learn what the job description consists of. Know where to go to get answers. If someone is there just to watch a desk and has no line of contact with the external customer, his or her position should be reviewed.

EXCUSE 84—HOLD WHILE I GO CHECK THE INVENTORY.

What should have happened: Let me check on that for you right now!

Insights: Use a wireless phone to maintain constant contact with the customer. If one is not available, ask if you can call the customer back with availability or briefly place them on hold. Let the customer make the final decision.

EXCUSE 85—I CAN'T HEAR YOU.

What should have happened: Would you repeat that please?

Insights: Remove as many distractions as possible. Take control of your work environment. Does it support what you're trying to accomplish with your customer service or detract from it? Don't be rude in the manner you express yourself to your customer. Be courteous throughout the conversation.

EXCUSE 86—HOLD ON. I'VE GOT TO GET A PEN.

What should have happened: May I take your order?

Insights: Always be prepared with the essential tools. Make it a habit at the beginning of the day to check your environment, not only your desk, but the office in general. Do you have adequate pens, pencils, and notepads? Is there paper in the fax machine? Is the computer working?

EXCUSE 87—I THOUGHT SOMEONE ELSE CALLED YOU BACK ON THAT.

What should have happened: Mr./Ms. _____, let me get that for you.

Insights: Get in the habit of following up with the customer as soon as you receive shipping data, etc. Don't wait for her to call you. Give an incredibly fast response time to every situation. Don't operate on hunches and feelings. Get the facts when it comes to dealing with your customer.

Wouldn't It Be Nice to Use Phrases Like These More Often with Our Customers

- How may I help you?
- We certainly look forward to doing business with you in the future.
- Yes we can!
- Thank you for the order!
- Please . . .
- Good morning/afternoon/evening!
- How are you today?
- Is there anything else I may help you with?
- How soon do you need this?
- Thank you for returning my call.
- May we get back to you on this?
- I appreciate your business.
- I'm happy to help you.
- Thank you for choosing us.
- I can do that for you.

- Let me take responsibility for that.
- May I check on that for you and give you a call back?
- May we please have your order?

EXCUSE 88—YES? OR YEH?

What should have happened: Good morning, this is _____. How may I help you?

Insights: It is important and reflects professionalism to have an appropriate greeting. Identify your company and yourself. Let the customer know that they have reached the right company—the company that is eager to give excellent service.

EXCUSE 89—HEY, FRED (ANY CUSTOMER'S NAME), WHAT CAN I DO FOR YOU?

What should have happened: Good morning, Mr. Moore, what can I do for you?

Insight: Don't offend the customer by being overly familiar without getting his or her approval. Let the customer establish when it is okay to be on a first-name basis. Until that is established, remain formal in your greeting and continued use of the customer's name.

EXCUSE 90—I DON'T KNOW IF THE SYSTEM WILL TAKE IT.

What should have happened: May I take your order?

Insights: Be supportive of the customer. Take the information. Know what the system's capabilities are before you take care of the customer. Uncertainty, a lack of confidence, and not believing you have what it takes to get the job done may make a customer uncomfortable, and he may question your ability to provide the quality service he is searching for.

EXCUSE 91—I DIDN'T SEE YOU COME IN.

What should have happened: Good afternoon/morning. What may I do for you (with a smile)?

Insights: You are there for the customer. Be alert. Be ready. Be prepared. When you miss a customer you miss an opportunity. Your awareness of your customer's whereabouts demonstrates your focus and ready to serve attitude.

Knowledge + Skills + Attitude = Professional Behavior

EXCUSE 92—IT'S SO EARLY AND I'M JUST NOT AWAKE YET.

What should have happened: How may I help you?

Insights: Get a cup of coffee, sprinkle your face with water, whatever is necessary to be alert before you begin your day so that you are ready to get into that

Your Customers Expect Excellent Service!

professional mode right away. How can you serve your customer if you are not alert? Don't miss important terms and details by not being top notch.

EXCUSE 93—WE REALLY DON'T HAVE ENOUGH PEOPLE HERE TO HELP TODAY.

What should have happened: Good morning, Mr./Ms. _____. How may I be of help today?

Insights: The customer depends on you. Give the exceptional service that is expected and required. Take the necessary information and call the customer back if you are not able to provide the service at that moment.

YOUR CUSTOMERS EXPECT EXCELLENT SERVICE!

EXCUSE 94—IT'S FRIDAY. YOU KNOW HOW THAT GOES.

What should have happened: How are you today Mr./Ms. _____? What may I do for you?

Insights: Be professional! The day of the week does not matter nor the time of day. The customer expects high quality professional responsive service upon request or she will take her business elsewhere. The way the customer should know "how it goes" is that it goes exceptionally well every day at your place of business and that she can expect the same high quality exceptional service no matter when she visits or calls.

EXCUSE 95—I'M REALLY UPSET WITH THE MANAGEMENT HERE.

What should have happened: How may I help you?

Insights: Be a professional. Your attitude affects your behavior with the customer. Don't allow yourself to become a victim and your professionalism to be influenced in a negative manner when it comes to your treatment of the customer.

EXCUSE 96—I JUST ENTERED THAT INTO THE COMPUTER.

What should have happened: May I pull that up on the computer and verify the details with you?

Insights: Entering information in the computer may be part of your job. That doesn't need to be told to the customer. Let your customer know about the service you will be providing for him and the actions you are taking on his behalf.

EXCUSE 97—HE DIDN'T PLACE YOUR ORDER INTO THE SYSTEM.

What should have happened: Let me check the status of your order.

Insights: If someone else did not complete the process, take the initiative to do so and follow through to be sure the customer is satisfied.

EXCUSE 98—YOU REALLY DON'T KNOW WHAT YOU WANT DO YOU?

What should have happened: May I ask you a few questions so that I can have a better understanding of what your need is and I can offer a solution. What is the application? Where will you be using this? Are you replacing or purchasing a new product?

Insights: Don't ever insult the customer or be condescending to her. She will take her business elsewhere. Be courteous throughout your meeting with a

Your Customers Demand Excellent Service!

customer. Be tactful and diplomatic as you ask exploratory questions to determine the exact item needed. This will allow you to be accurate and thorough in servicing your customer.

EXCUSE 99—I SORT OF LOST THAT CUSTOMER WHEN I TRIED TO TRANSFER HIM.

What should have happened: Let me transfer you to the individual who will assist you. If you do experience any problems, you can reach me at _____ . My name is

_____ .

Insights: Anticipate and be prepared for any problems that may surface. Know your phone

---

system. Know the process for transferring. Notice that this particular excuse is one given to an internal customer. We are truly customers unto each other and have a significant impact either directly or indirectly each day in the workplace on others.

EXCUSE 100—YOU'VE CALLED THE WRONG DEPARTMENT/AREA.

What should have happened: May I have your name and phone number? I will have someone from that department call you, or if you prefer, I can transfer you.

Insights: Assist the customer and follow through to be sure he gets to the proper department or person.

EXCUSE 101—I'M IN TRAINING.

What should have happened: How may I help you?

Insights: Convey confidence. Part of your training is to practice your delivery of excellent service. While in training each encounter

Why Don't You Do These things?

is a learning experience. As Vince Lombardi said, "It's not practice that makes perfect, it's perfect practice that makes perfect." Always be aware of the image you are placing in the customer's mind.

EXCUSE 102—I'M JUST HERE TO ANSWER THE PHONE. CAN YOU CALL BACK IN ABOUT 45 MINUTES?

What should have happened: May I have your name, phone number, and an explanation of what you need, and I will have someone call you back.

Insights: Don't lose the customer. If you cannot service her at the time she calls, you may be sending her to the competition. Tell her what you can do for her and be certain to follow through.

EXCUSE 103—IT'S MY FIRST DAY.

What should have happened: How may I help you today?

Insights: Your customer doesn't care if it is your first day or your last day. He wants service. Even though it is your first day on the

EXCELLENT SERVICE EXCELLENT SERVICE EXCELLENT SERVICE

YOUR CUSTOMERS DEMAND EXCELLENT SERVICE!

EXCELLENT SERVICE EXCELLENT SERVICE EXCELLENT SERVICE

WHY DON'T YOU DO THESE THINGS?

job, be as professional as you possibly can be. Use your supervisor or co-worker when necessary for correct information, procedures, etc. It is important to make your job look easy, like you have been doing it for a long time.

EXCUSE 104—I DIDN'T KNOW WE OFFERED/PROVIDED/DID/ SERVICED THAT.

What should have happened: May I take your order please?

Insights: Ask questions until you have the complete details of what the customer is requesting. Once you are able to research the order, be sure to keep notes for future reference in case it comes up again. You will be able to service the next customer even better.

EXCUSE 105—THESE ARE NOT HARD QUESTIONS I AM ASKING YOU.

What should have happened: Let's review these questions again so that I may fully understand your needs and assist you.

Insights: Don't insult or mistreat the customer by asking improper questions or making insulting remarks. It may seem very simple to you; but if the customer is not familiar with the product or service, he may need some patience, guidance, and attention in order to determine his situation accurately. Accept your customer's confusion as an opportunity. You have the responsibility to educate your customer to the quality of the service you can provide.

EXCUSE 106—EXCUSE ME FOR NOT BEING CLAIRVOYANT.

What should have happened: How may I help you Ms./Mr. _____? Allow me to ask you a few questions so that I may best understand how to take care of your needs.

Insights: Customers don't expect you to be a mind reader or psychic. Take the necessary steps to find out exactly what the customer is shopping for. Ask as many questions as possible to identify each detail. Avoid mistakes that could happen later by making the appropriate investment in time and attention at the start. Be certain not to be insulting or condescending to the customer.

EXCUSE 107—YOUR ORDER WENT TO THE WRONG LOCATION.

What should have happened: Let me check on the status of your order and call you right back.

Insights: Tell the customer what action you are going to take and then do just that. Keep the customer informed and continue to inform her of how you are being responsive to her needs.

EXCUSE 108—YOUR ORDER SORT OF GOT LOST.

What should have happened: I'm going to personally track your order and find out exactly what the status of it is. Let me please take your information and I will call you back.

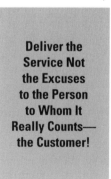

Deliver the Service Not the Excuses to the Person to Whom It Really Counts— the Customer!

Insights: Again, the focus needs to be on what action is going to take place to service the customer and fulfill the customer's needs.

EXCUSE 109—I CAN RAISE MY VOICE JUST AS LOUD AS YOURS.

What should have happened: How may I help you?

Insights: When you're dealing with an angry or irate customer, it's often tempting to join in the loud talk and angry behavior yourself. It takes a great deal of professionalism to remain calm while your customer vents and dumps his bucket so to speak. By using active listening skills while remaining calm yourself, you are assisting your customer in getting control of his own anger and becoming rational. Once you accomplish that, you can address the customer's problem and fulfill his needs.

EXCUSE 110—THE DELIVERY SERVICE DIDN'T COME THROUGH, AND YOUR ORDER IS DELAYED.

What should have happened: I'll check on the status of your order and call you back with a report.

Insights: Look into it, and get the shipping information. Letting the customer know what you can do will put her more at ease and allow her to see that your goal is to resolve her problem and not add to it.

YOU ARE IN THE NEEDS FULFILLMENT BUSINESS!

EXCUSE 111—SOMEONE SHOULD BE ABLE TO HELP YOU IN ABOUT 45 MINUTES; THEY'RE IN A MEETING.

What should have happened: May I please take your name and number and have someone call you or may I help you?

Insights: Meetings are important, but nothing should cause you to take your focus off of the customer. If you meet to improve your skills while ignoring the customer, you may not have a customer to return to when you decide to come back. You need to do both: continuously improve knowledge and skills while focusing on customer needs.

EXCUSE 112—IT'S MONDAY AND I'M NOT AWAKE YET.

What should have happened: How may I help you?

Insights: Get into that professional mode and deliver excellent service at all times. Accept the responsibility that comes with the position. You need to be alert and display enthusiasm whenever you deal with a customer. Sleepiness and lack of attention is often interpreted as a lack of concern and caring, resulting in your customer taking his business elsewhere.

TAKE A MOMENT AND TRY NOT TO REACT BUT TO RESPOND TO YOUR CUSTOMERS AND THEIR NEEDS.

Common Sense Still Goes a Long Way When Dealing with a Customer

- Have a smile on your face.
- Nod periodically during communication.
- Lean forward toward the customer slightly.
- Maintain eye contact.
- Give your full attention and listen carefully.
- Have a pleasant, clean appearance.
- Use good posture.
- Have a specific statement you use when you answer the phone. It should identify your company, yourself, and your department.
- Use the customer's name frequently.
- Be courteous.
- Speak clearly using enunciation.
- Have a pleasant tone of voice.
- Display enthusiasm for your work.
- Focus on the customer.
- Remove as many distractions as possible.

EXCUSE 113—YOU STILL DON'T KNOW WHAT YOU WANT DO YOU?

What should have happened: How may I help you? May I ask you a few questions so that I may best assist you?

Insights: The responsibility is on your shoulders to educate your customer both tactfully and diplomatically to the quality of what you have to offer. Sometimes this can be a real challenge, but the rewards can be incredible for both you and the customer. This excuse should never have occurred the first time (Excuse 98).

EXCUSE 114—WE'VE GOT A REAL FIRE HERE WE'RE TRYING TO PUT OUT, AND I REALLY CAN'T HELP YOU RIGHT NOW.

What should have happened: May I please take your information, name, and number and call you back?

Insights: So many companies feel like they are constantly putting out fires, always moving from one trauma to the next. What a terribly reactive environment to function in. High stress, high anxiety must be the norm. You must be able to anticipate change and customer needs. As a professional, this will allow you to build customer-responsive relationships (the major focus in *The New Sales Game*) and to move from being only a provider of services to becoming a solutions provider for your

> "If you're not enthusiastic about your customers and their business, someone else will be."

customers. It doesn't just make life easier for the customer but also for you. You become so valuable to the customer that it is rare when he thinks of taking his business to another provider.

EXCUSE 115—THERE IS A JOB AHEAD OF YOURS THAT IS TAKING LONGER THAN EXPECTED.

What should have happened: Please allow me to gather the information on your project and call you right back with a status report.

Insights: The customer doesn't care if there are five or fifty other jobs ahead of his, he wants his work done and delivered in the agreed upon time. Don't focus on any other project or customer other than the one you are dealing with at that moment. Tell him what you can do for him and gather your forces to make every effort to do what you said you were going to do. Your reputation for honesty and integrity may be on the line. Don't ever make promises you know you cannot keep or deliver. It will come back to hurt your business internally and externally.

EXCUSE 116—THE EQUIPMENT IS NOT WORKING PROPERLY.

What should have happened: How may I help you?

Insights: What image of your organization are you placing in the mind of the customer? Be careful! What you say to the customer should be thought about prior to speaking. It can take years to build a strong customer-responsive relationship and it can be destroyed quickly as the result of a brief moment of poorly chosen words. Emphasize the positives; let your customer know what you can do for her and then do it!

EXCUSE 117—IF YOU WOULD BRING UP OUR WEB PAGE, YOU WILL FIND THAT INFORMATION.

What should have happened: Let me find that for you sir/madam.

Insights: When the customer has a need, take care of it! Be careful how you inform him/her of options available. Don't use the web site as a catchall or pass along and thus avoid customer contact and service. Remember, no matter how far the technology advances, it is only part of the solution. the "Human Factor" is people dealing with people and that should take precedence and be done in a tactful manner.

THERE SHOULD BE NO EXCUSES FOR NOT DELIVERING EXCELLENT CUSTOMER SERVICE.

We Would Like to Hear from You

We would like to hear from you. Please share with us the excuses you have heard for not delivering excellent customer service. List them below with your comments (you are welcome to e-mail them to us). We would enjoy any other success stories, concerns, questions, etc., you may wish to share within the realm of customer service. Thank you,

Darryl S. Doane and Rose D. Sloat
e-mail: DJourn@aol.com

Excuse:

_____

_____

Comments, observations, or questions:

_____

_____

Excuse:

_____

_____

_____

_____

Comments, observations, or questions:

_____

_____

Acknowledgments

We would like to acknowledge the contributions of the following people during the development of this book.

Joe Breniser, President, Creative Training Institute, who over the years has been a friend, mentor, co-worker, and inspiration to us. Joe is one of the individuals who has had a dramatic impact on us and the early development of our company. We thank him for reviewing the manuscript of *Excuses, Excuses, Excuses, . . .* and discussing his feelings with us regarding the text.

Barbara Doane, for sharing comments with us that eventually evolved into the "You Can't Put It Back" story.

Jerry Drake, Business Manager for Liquid Control Corporation, for his review of the manuscript and the correction of a quote. We are grateful for his friendship and encouragement.

Diane Erickson, Director of Special Projects, Danner Press, for her review of the manuscript and insightful comments.

The many Customer Service and Sales Representatives, both Inside and Outside Sales People, who have shared their stories, concerns, ideas, escapades, and dreams with us over the past five years. You have been an inspiration!

There Should Be No Excuses for Not Delivering Excellent Customer Service.

About the Authors

Darryl S. Doane and Rose D. Sloat are the owners of The Learning Service, Ltd., located in Canton, Ohio. They are independent performance-based training consultants. The Learning Service, Ltd. specializes in customer service and sales training; managerial and leadership skills development; time mastery; communication skills; performance coaching; and customizing programs specifically suited to an organization's identified needs. "We believe that an organization's success depends upon the performance of its people. Our programs impact performance by supplying the necessary tools for individuals to change their own behavior."

Darryl S. Doane

Darryl has served as a teacher, speaker, facilitator, and professional consultant for over 20 years. He has presented outstanding programs to numerous organizations including adult, college, youth organizations, corporations, churches, and civic groups. He has worked with national organizations such as the National Association of Student Councils and Secondary Schools Principals and was a participant in NASA's Teacher in Space Program. He served as Senior Training Specialist for a billion-dollar corporation for seven years prior to beginning his own business. Darryl is coauthor of *The New Sales Game*.

Rose D. Sloat

Rose served as the Training Coordinator of a billion-dollar company for fifteen years. She has learned, taught, and applied every component within the training arena from organizing and scheduling training to writing and producing learning events. Rose's expertise in paying "attention to detail" has enabled The Learning Service, Ltd. to become an effective and efficient means of quality learning for companies who have chosen to outsource their training needs. Rose's co-authoring of *The New Sales Game* with Darryl represents an opportunity to share over 20 years of sales and customer-responsive service experiences.

The New Sales Game©

The New Sales Game is a highly interactive, facilitated program that uses presentations, group discussion, and a variety of activities to help your sales force **achieve the next level** of sales success.

Participants will learn how to:

- Bring their entire sales force (rookies, those with middle of the road years of experience, and seasoned veterans) together in a unified focus and direction

- Focus on the real needs and perceptions of their customers

- Determine your company's value-added services

- Proactively become solution providers

Material includes a comprehensive Leader's Guide with clear objectives, a complete course outline, a detailed script, questions and answers, and overhead transparency masters making it simple for sales managers or trainers to facilitate the program. The *New Sales Game* is an easy-to-deliver one-day program that will energize and add a powerful new dimension to your sales meetings.